GIANTS OF SCIENCE

Jonas Salk

Polio Vaccine Pioneer

Peggy J. Parks

BLACKBIRCH™
PRESS

San Diego • Detroit • New York • San Francisco • Cleveland
New Haven, Conn. • Waterville, Maine • London • Munich

THOMSON
✳
GALE™

© 2004 by Blackbirch Press™. Blackbirch Press™ is an imprint of The Gale Group, Inc., a division of Thomson Learning, Inc.

Blackbirch Press™ and Thomson Learning™ are trademarks used herein under license.

For more information, contact
The Gale Group, Inc.
27500 Drake Rd.
Farmington Hills, MI 48331-3535
Or you can visit our Internet site at http://www.gale.com

Photo Credits: cover © Eddie Adams/CORBIS SYGMA; pg. 4 © Photo Disc; pg. 5 © CORBIS; pg. 6, 49 © CDC - National Center for Disease Control; pg. 10 © CDC/ Dr. Karp, Emory University; pg. 7 © Time Life Pictures/Getty Images; pg. 9, 11-13, 18-19, 26, 29, 35, 41, 43, 44, 46-48, 52, 56, 59 © Bettmann/CORBIS; pg. 15 © Charles E. Rotkin/CORBIS; pg. 22 © Ron Boardman; Frank Land Picture Agency/CORBIS; pg. 21 © Museum of the City of New York/CORBIS; pg. 24 © Howard Sochurek/CORBIS; pg. 55 © Peter Aprahamina/CORBIS; pg. 57 © AFP/Getty Images; pg. 32, 34, 39, 50 © Hulton|Archive/Getty Images; pg. 33 © R. Green/Photo Researchers; pg. 16, 27, 30 © Library of Congress; pg. 23 © FDR Library; pg. 37 © National Archives; pg 38 © Al Fenn/Time Life Pictures/Getty Images

LIBRARY OF CONGRESS CATALOGING-IN-PUBLICATION DATA

Parks, Peggy J., 1951-
   Jonas Salk / by Peggy J. Parks.
      p. cm. — (Giants of science)
Summary: A biography of the scientist and humanitarian who discovered the vaccine for polio, a disease which crippled many people in the early part of the twentieth century. Includes bibliographical references and index.
   ISBN 1-56711-475-X
   1. Salk, Jonas, 1914—Juvenile literature. 2. Virologists—United States—Biography—Juvenile literature. 3. Poliomyelitis vaccine—Juvenile literature. [1. Salk, Jonas, 1914- 2. Physicians. 3. Scientists. 4. Poliomyelitis vaccine.] I. Title. II. Series.

   QR31.S25P37 2003
   610'.92--dc21

                                                                    2003004504

2

Printed in China
10 9 8 7 6 5 4 3 2 1

CONTENTS

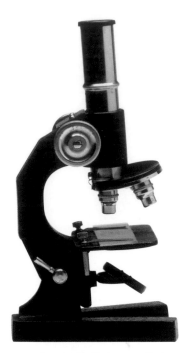

Conquering a Deadly Disease

In the summer of 1952, an American scientific researcher named Jonas Salk made an amazing medical breakthrough. He had developed a vaccine against poliomyelitis, more commonly known as polio. Americans had long lived in fear of polio, the devastating disease that crippled or killed thousands of people, most of whom were young adults and children. A vaccine that could prevent polio was desperately needed. After many years of research and experiments, Salk believed his vaccine would be effective. Now all he needed to do was prove it.

Jonas Salk (opposite) examined blood samples under a microscope (above) to verify the effectiveness of his polio vaccine.

To test his vaccine, Salk injected it into live, healthy monkeys that were not infected with polio. After a waiting period, he drew blood from the animals and then checked it under a microscope. As he had hoped, the blood samples showed that antibodies in the animals' blood were higher than they had been before the vaccine. These antibodies, which acted as natural disease-fighting agents, were created by the monkeys' immune systems in response to the vaccine. From this, Salk could tell that the vaccine was effective—but there was no guarantee that it would also work on people. The only way to find out was to do experimental tests on humans.

Salk decided to perform the tests on children at the D.T. Watson Home for Crippled Children, which was located near

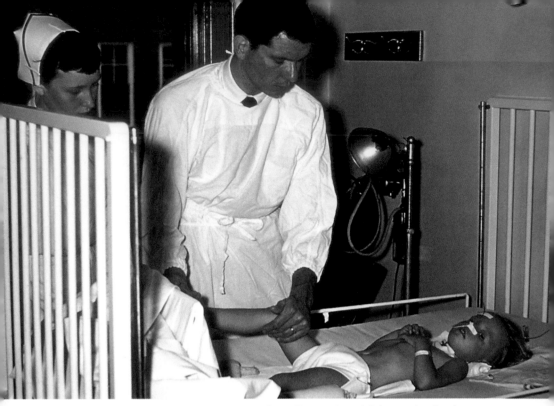

Because they could not catch polio again, children who had already had the disease were the ideal first test subjects for Salk's vaccine.

Pittsburgh, Pennsylvania. The children who would participate had already had polio, so they were not at risk of catching it again. Their parents were very much in favor of the experiment, as were doctors and nurses at the home. They knew that if the vaccine worked, it could protect other children and end a crippling, deadly disease.

The test was kept totally secret from the public because it was still just an experiment—there was no way to know if the vaccine would actually be effective. One medical scientist, quoted in the book *Breakthrough: The Saga of Jonas Salk*, explains why this secrecy was so important: "You can't do pioneer human experimentation effectively without it. The news is too exciting. It gets into the newspapers. Your phone begins ringing and does not stop. Part of the public goes haywire with premature [hope] and the rest with unwarranted fear. Do-gooders and crackpots of all shapes and sizes try to get into the act, interfering with the selection of experimental subjects and making the terms and conditions of the experiment a matter for public debate." [1]

On June 12, 1952, Salk went to the Watson Home and drew blood samples from forty-five children. He then returned to his laboratory and examined the blood under a microscope. His intent was to find out what types of antibodies the children had, and how much of these antibodies were in their blood. His next step would be to vaccinate the children, and then retest their blood to see if their antibodies had increased.

A few weeks later, Salk returned to the Watson Home to inject the children with his experimental vaccine. He was confident that the children were immune to polio, and he firmly believed that his vaccine was safe. Yet he could not help feeling nervous, as he later explained: "When you inoculate [vaccinate] children with a polio vaccine, you don't sleep well for two or three months." [2] In the following days and weeks, he telephoned and visited the home frequently. None of the children suffered any side effects from the vaccine. Salk then went one step further. He injected his vaccine into children who did not have any antibodies in their blood. This was risky because unlike the children who previously had polio, these children had the potential to develop it. Afterwards, however, not one of them displayed any symptoms of the disease.

A cover of Time *magazine features Jonas Salk. The scientist kept his experiment secret from the public until its completion.*

Toward the end of the summer, Salk saw the results for which he had hoped. An examination of the children's blood showed higher levels of antibodies in those who already had polio. It also showed that antibodies had developed in the children who did not have polio. He then combined the antibodies with live samples of poliovirus. The virus was destroyed, which proved that his vaccine was not only safe, but it was also capable of protecting children from polio. This was an incredible discovery that could mean the end of a terrible disease. Salk later commented that seeing the results of his experiment before his eyes was the thrill of his life.

A Mysterious Epidemic

Salk's vaccine brought an end to a disease that had ravaged the United States for many years. The first American outbreak was in Vermont in the 1890s. This was not considered an epidemic, or major outbreak of the disease, because only 132 people caught it. During the summer of 1916, however, tragedy struck New York City. A major polio epidemic broke out, and it quickly spread to other mid-Atlantic states. At first, scientists and doctors were mystified because no one knew what the disease was. It almost always struck during the hot months of summer. Most cases involved children, and those who became ill often had symptoms that were similar to a cold, including headaches, chills, joint stiffness, and sore throats. Some of these victims became paralyzed in their arms, legs, or entire bodies. Those who suffered paralysis of the muscles needed for breathing or swallowing often died.

By the middle of August 1916, almost nine thousand cases of the mysterious illness had been reported in the eastern states. Scientists identified it as poliomyelitis, a disease that attacks the body's nervous system. Poliomyelitis had existed for hundreds of years, but outbreaks of it were rare. Never before in history had it struck so many people so quickly. Before the summer of 1916 ended, nearly thirty thousand cases of polio, including six thousand deaths, had been reported in twenty-six states. Health officials knew they faced a major crisis. Still, the epidemic continued to rage on, and there seemed to be no end

Children were most susceptible to the major polio epidemic that struck the mid Atlantic states in 1916. That summer, six thousand people died from polio.

in sight. Author Kathryn Black wrote: "Fear hung like heat in the summer. No one knew how you got it. Did you breathe it in, swallow it in contaminated milk, drink it down at a public fountain, or get it from flies on your picnic lunch?"[3]

Early Polio Research

Long before the 1916 epidemic, scientists had begun to research polio's causes and effects. After several outbreaks in Europe in the 1800s, German and Swedish physicians studied the disease. They determined that it attacked a person's nervous system, primarily the spinal cord, and that it could result in paralysis or death.

In the early 1900s, European medical researchers concluded that polio was a form of virus, or a tiny organism that could lead to disease. They also determined that it was highly contagious, and that it was spread through person-to-person contact. As they continued to study polio, they found that patients who were stricken with it, and had recovered from it, almost never caught it again. This was because of the antibodies their immune systems had created in response to the infection. With that in mind, researchers believed the way to protect people was to inject them with a tiny amount of the virus—just enough to cause the formation of antibodies.

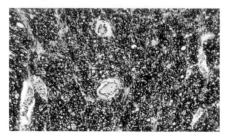

In the 1800s, European scientists determined that polio attacked the spinal cord and caused degeneration, as shown in this magnified image.

In 1935, an American doctor named John Kolmer developed an experimental vaccine. He used chemicals to weaken the poliovirus, but he did not use enough to kill it. He tested the vaccine on monkeys, and then he inoculated himself and members of his family. When they did not get sick, Kolmer became confident that his vaccine was safe. He distributed it to hundreds of physicians, who then used it to inoculate children. The results were tragic. Even though the virus had been weakened, it was still strong enough to cause polio in some of the children. A number of children died, and others were left paralyzed.

When the American people heard about Kolmer's experiment, they became very frightened. Many people not only feared polio, they also feared the vaccines that were developed to prevent it.

Salk Gets Involved

Salk became interested in the poliovirus during the 1940s. As head of a research laboratory at the University of Pittsburgh, he began to study and experiment with the virus. By 1952, he had developed the first version of his polio vaccine and was ready to see if it worked. The tests he performed at the Watson Home in the summer of 1952 proved that his vaccine was not only safe, but it could also prevent polio.

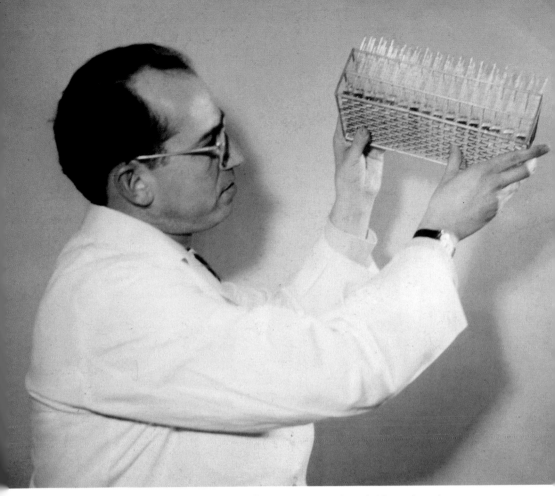

Salk first began work on a polio vaccine in the 1940s, when he headed a research laboratory at the University of Pennsylvania.

Salk was not the first scientist to research the poliovirus, nor was he the first to experiment with vaccines. He was, however, the first to be successful. The story of Jonas Salk—the medical scientist who became known as "The Man Who Saved the Children"—began in New York City, where he was born and raised.

Family Life

Jonas Edward Salk was born on October 28, 1914, in the East Harlem section of New York City. His parents, Daniel and Dora (Dolly) Salk, were Jewish immigrants from Russia who had very little education. Daniel Salk, a designer of ladies' blouses for the garment industry, had finished elementary school but never graduated from high school. Dolly Salk was a home-maker who had no schooling, but who was an ambitious, hardworking woman.

Daniel and Dolly had three sons: Jonas, Herman, and Lee. Dolly favored Jonas, who was her oldest, but she loved all her sons, and she wanted the best for them. Because she wanted their lives to be better than her own, she was determined for them to pursue a formal education. She provided a nurturing home environment, and encouraged hard work so her sons could succeed at whatever path they chose to follow. She was particularly certain that Jonas would someday accomplish great things. He later said that his mother constantly challenged him and pushed him to live up to his potential.

As a child, Jonas had a natural curiosity, especially about anything that related to human beings. He once said that he had been curious from the time he was very young: "There was a photograph of me when I was a year old, and there was that look of curiosity on that infant's face. . . . I have the suspicion that this curiosity was very much a part of my early life: asking questions about unreasonableness. I tended to observe, and reflect and wonder. That sense of wonder, I think, is built into us."[4]

A biography of biologist Louis Pasteur (pictured) greatly influenced young Jonas.

Schooling in New York

When Jonas was a young boy, his family moved to an apartment in another area of New York City called the Bronx. He attended school along with other children of immigrants, and while he got along well with his classmates, he was not very outgoing. In fact, he was a quiet boy who spent more time alone than he did socializing with other children.

During his early school years, Jonas was a bright, motivated student. He was not, however, enthusiastic about reading, and most of the reading he did was related to schoolwork. Later in life he could recall only two books that had been significant to him when he was young: one about the life of the famous biologist Louis Pasteur, and one titled *The Island Within.* Yet even though he did not spend much time reading, Jonas did spend a great deal of time thinking about the world around him and the humans who lived in it.

Salk became interested in science when enrolled at the City College of New York (pictured).

In 1928, Jonas was accepted into Townsend Harris Hall High School. This was a preparatory school that was run by the City College of New York, and it was reserved for only the most gifted and promising students. Jonas excelled at Townsend Harris, and like all his classmates, he completed his studies in three years rather than four. After his graduation in 1931, he entered City College.

From Law to Medicine

Salk's original plan was to become a lawyer, so he entered the college's pre-law program. He knew his mother did not think he would make a good lawyer because, as he later admitted, he could not ever seem to win an argument with her. She wanted him to become a teacher, but he was not interested in a teaching career. He thought that by being a lawyer, he would be able to fight injustice.

Not long after he started college, Salk lost interest in becoming a lawyer. This was because something else had captured his attention: the world of science. The more he studied chemistry, biology, and other sciences, the more he saw the importance of scientific research. Also, it became clear to him that scientists had the freedom to make discoveries based on their own personal theories. From that point on, there was no question about what he wanted to do with his life. His dream was to have a career that somehow involved both science and medicine, and he changed his college major to premedical studies.

In June 1934, Salk graduated from college with a bachelor of science degree and applied to New York University School of Medicine. His alternative plan, if he were not accepted, was to enter graduate school to study endocrinology, a specialty related to internal glands and diseases. Salk was accepted by the university, though, and at the age of nineteen he began his medical studies.

Although he studied to become a doctor, Salk did not plan to practice medicine. Rather, he wanted to become a medical scientist. He felt this was the best way to fulfill his desire to help humankind and do something that would make a positive difference in the world. He dreamed of someday making medical discoveries that would benefit people.

The Turning Point

At the end of Salk's first year at New York University, Dr. R. Keith Cannan, a chemistry professor, asked to see him. Salk had been an excellent student, but he was worried about why Cannan wanted to meet with him. He thought the professor might tell him that he was failing. Actually, the opposite was true. Cannan offered Salk an opportunity to take a leave of absence from his studies and spend a year in biochemistry research, which involved studying the chemistry of living things. This was an intriguing idea for Salk. From the time he first entered medical school, he had wanted to focus on scientific research. Yet it was a difficult decision for him. It meant

After earning his bachelor's degree, Salk attended the School of Medicine at New York University (pictured) with plans to become a medical scientist.

that he would have to leave his class, and then return a year later to an unfamiliar class. After thinking carefully about it, he decided to accept Cannan's offer because he believed it would help him accomplish his goals.

The year was not an especially productive one for Salk, who later admitted that he did not get very much work done. It was beneficial for him, though, because he learned about a new area of science: the study of viruses and the immune system. He had not been exposed to this before, and he later remarked that the year was a turning point in his life: "Risks, I like to say, always pay off. You learn what to do, or what not to do. . . .If I had failed to take advantage of that opportunity, I would not have known what I would have missed. That was the beginning of many similar opportunities which have come my way."[5]

15

While still in medical school, Salk challenged the belief that vaccines made from toxoids, used to prevent diphtheria, were not effective against viral diseases.

Doubting Established Beliefs

Salk completed his year of research in 1936 and returned to his medical studies. During his second year of medical school, he discovered something that helped shape his future—his refusal to accept common beliefs about medical science when he felt those beliefs were wrong.

In a class lecture, Salk heard that vaccines made with chemically treated toxins (traces of a disease) could protect against such deadly illnesses as diphtheria and tetanus. The chemicals inactivated, or killed, the toxins so they were no longer infectious. These killed toxins, known as toxoids, could then be used to make vaccines that built antibodies in people's blood, and protected them against disease.

In another lecture, however, he heard something quite different. This lecture dealt with viruses. Salk was told that in order to develop immunity against a viral disease, someone had to first have the disease—that it was not possible to become immune through the use of killed viruses. He found this very odd, as he later explained: "What struck me was that both statements couldn't be true. And I asked why this was so, and the answer that was given was in a sense, 'Because.' There was no satisfactory answer. . . . It didn't make sense and that question persisted in my mind."[6]

This contradiction bothered Salk. He wondered, if a killed toxin could fight a bacterial disease such as diphtheria, why would that same principle not apply to a viral disease? He did not challenge his professor's statement, though, and he later explained why: "For all I knew, he was right, even though he sounded wrong. I gave the matter a lot of thought for years, began testing it at the first opportunity, and learned that my early suspicions had been well founded."[7]

A Mentor and a Friend

During his last year of medical school, Salk received the highest honor that could be achieved by medical students: He was named to Alpha Omega Alpha, an esteemed medical honor society. It was also during that final year that he had a chance to work with Dr. Thomas Francis Jr., a highly respected scientist who was chairman of the school's bacteriology department.

Francis had earned a name for himself through his studies of viruses, particularly the influenza virus. At that time, influenza posed a grave risk and was considered one of the world's most deadly diseases. A pandemic, or worldwide epidemic, of Spanish influenza had occurred in 1918, when World War I was still in progress. The disease had started in the United States, and in just a few short months, it had spread throughout the world. More than 20 million people died, and more than a half-million of them were Americans. Francis had devoted a great deal of time to studying the influenza virus. Salk was interested in working with him, and he wanted to learn more about influenza research. Plus, there was another reason Salk was eager to work with Francis: They shared the same viewpoint about live versus killed viruses in vaccinations.

In 1918, a worldwide epidemic of Spanish influenza spread across the globe and killed 20 million people.

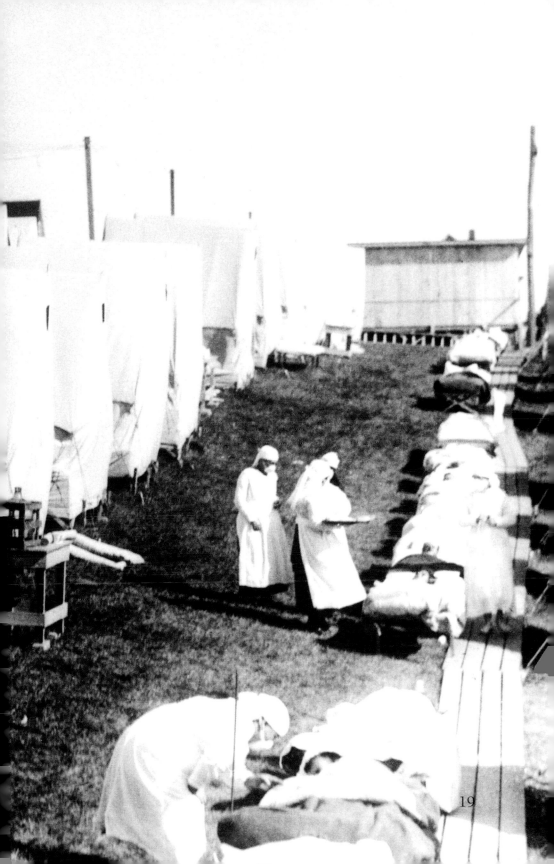

Together, Salk and Francis performed experiments in the laboratory. They grew the influenza virus and used chemicals or radiation to make it inactive. Then they tested the results. As they continued their research and experiments, they discovered that their belief had been correct: An inactive virus could indeed provide immunity against a viral disease. They developed a close working relationship and Francis became Salk's mentor, as well as his good friend.

After Medical School

Salk developed another relationship during his last year at New York University. That was when he met his future wife, Donna Lindsay. A graduate student at the New York School of Social Work, Lindsay was an attractive and highly intelligent woman who described Salk this way: "He was a good dancer, an amusing and exciting conversationalist, and as different from the stereotype of the one-track scientist as anyone could possibly be."[8] In June 1939, Salk graduated with a doctor of medicine degree from New York University School of Medicine. The next day after his graduation, he and Lindsay were married at West End Synagogue in New York.

Over the following months, Salk continued to work with Francis on influenza research. Then in March 1940, Salk went to New York City's Mount Sinai Hospital to do his internship. His acceptance into Mount Sinai was significant because there was heavy competition for internships. Out of the 250 medical school graduates who applied, only twelve were accepted. One distinguished physician who supervised Salk during this time described him as the best intern at the hospital—the most mature, the most reliable, and someone who never got flustered under pressure: "He worked under me for a while and it was like having another self. You told him to do something and it got done. It got done and so did a dozen things you hadn't thought of."[9] Eventually, Salk was elected president of the house staff by the other Mount Sinai interns and residents. In this position, he supervised the newer interns and was regarded as a patient, caring mentor by everyone who reported to him.

In 1940, Salk began a coveted internship at Mount Sinai Hospital in New York and impressed doctors there with his skill in surgery.

During his internship, Salk performed the usual duties of a physician. He saw patients and diagnosed illnesses, and his talent at performing surgery impressed other surgeons at the hospital. Still, his future career goals did not change. He planned to be a medical scientist rather than a practicing physician, and he spent as much time as possible in the laboratory. He also stayed in close touch with Francis, who had moved to Ann Arbor, Michigan, to work at the University of Michigan School of Public Health.

Leaving New York

Francis's new position was head of the school's epidemiology department, which focused on the study of disease. Much of his time was devoted to influenza research. Toward the end of Salk's internship, he went to visit Francis to seek his advice. New York had always been home to Salk, and he wanted to stay there, but he was not able to find work as a medical researcher. He applied for positions at several New York institutions, but he had been turned down. He suspected that this was largely because he was Jewish; discrimination against Jewish people was common at that time. Whatever the reason, Salk was bitterly disappointed. He thought that Francis, his mentor and friend, might be able to help him.

Salk told Francis that he wanted to continue his research in viral diseases. His intent was to work in a research laboratory for a few months and then join Francis at the University of Michigan. Francis supported his decision. After Salk went back to New York, Francis wrote letters to several institutions on his behalf, to help him find a position.

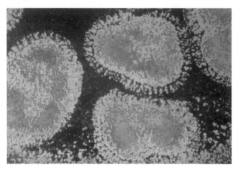

Salk researched the influenza virus (above) for an organization founded by polio survivor Franklin D. Roosevelt (opposite).

When Salk completed his internship in 1942, he changed his plans and started working immediately with Francis. By that time, World War II had broken out, and there was a crucial need for an influenza vaccine. No one had forgotten how many people died as a result of the influenza outbreak during the last world war, and nearly fifty thousand of those victims had been American soldiers. The need for an influenza vaccine had become a matter of national urgency.

In April 1942, Salk and his wife moved to Michigan, where they rented an old farmhouse in a rural area near Ann Arbor. Donna Salk went to work as a social worker, and Salk went to work with Francis at the University of Michigan School of Public Health.

Influenza Research

Salk's position was known as a fellowship, and it was made possible by a grant from the National Foundation for Infantile Paralysis. The organization was primarily devoted to polio research and had been founded by President Franklin Roosevelt, who was a polio victim. The foundation funded

other types of research as well, and Salk's assignment was to focus on influenza.

Salk was eager to begin his work, and Francis was equally excited to have Salk in his laboratory, as he explained: "Jonas was a blessing in those days. Workers with his initiative and talent were even scarcer than usual because of the war, but our scientific opportunities and responsibilities were more pressing. Someone willing to take hold, as Jonas was could move ahead rapidity. . . . It was a busy time, the pressure was on, and Jonas fit right in."[10]

Salk's laboratory experiments revolved around influenza virus research and testing experimental vaccines. He knew that immunity to a disease depend-ed on the amount of anti-bodies that were in the blood— the higher the antibodies, the greater the immunity. He and Francis experimented with killed viruses, and they found that vaccines made with them produced the same amount of antibodies as those made with live viruses. This discovery led Salk and Francis to develop an effective killed-virus influenza vaccine.

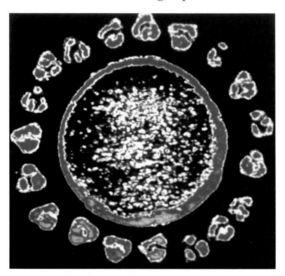

Salk studied how vaccines affected antibodies (pictured) and, with Dr. Thomas Francis, developed an influenza vaccine.

In 1943, Salk began to work with the U.S. Army Influenza Commission. The group, whose goal was to prevent another outbreak of influenza among the armed forces, was aware of Salk's reputation. During his time in Ann Arbor, he had become known as an expert on influenza. That same year, Salk traveled to military bases, such as Fort Custer in Michigan and Fort Dix in New Jersey, and tested the influenza vaccine in massive field trials. Thousands of soldiers received the vaccination. It was effective and considered a major success.

The next few years were eventful for Salk. He and his wife became parents in 1944, when their son Peter was born. The following year, after the end of World War II, Salk was sent to Germany to help organize diagnostic laboratories for the prevention of influenza epidemics. He felt honored that out of everyone who worked with the influenza commission, he was the one selected to go. He found the trip very worthwhile, and he enjoyed his work in Europe.

The Quest for Independence

When Salk returned home, he began to consider leaving his position at the University of Michigan. He had become more independent, and his ideas about influenza did not always agree with those of his mentor. He was promoted to an assistant professor position in 1946, but he still considered moving on. His relationship with Francis had grown strained, and he yearned for a laboratory where he could be in charge and make his own decisions. He explored opportunities in California, Ohio, and New York, but was unable to find the type of position he wanted.

In early 1947, Salk heard about an opportunity that appealed to him. The University of Pittsburgh School of Medicine was looking for someone to head up its virus research laboratory. The school was also pursuing polio research, which had begun to interest Salk. There was one problem, though. The school did not have a good reputation among medical scientists because it devoted almost no money to research. In addition, most of its professors were full-time doctors who only taught on the side. It did not help the school's image that it was located in Pittsburgh, which, at that time, was a dirty, polluted city. The school was said to be dirty as well.

Salk gave this a great deal of thought. He had his family to consider, especially with the recent birth of his second son,

Salk's position as head of his own research laboratory at the University of Pittsburgh gave the scientist the freedom he needed to begin polio research.

Derrell. He also heard strong objections from Francis and others, who tried to convince him that moving to Pittsburgh would be a mistake. Salk, however, saw it as an excellent chance to become independent. He also thought it would allow him the freedom to develop his own virus research program, as he later explained: "The opportunity in Pittsburgh was something that others did not see, and I was advised against doing something as foolish as that because there was so little there. However, I did see that there was an opportunity to do two things. One was to continue the work I was doing on influenza, and two, to begin to work on polio."[11] After one visit to the school, Salk accepted the university's offer to become a research professor and head of the virus research laboratory.

A New Start

Salk, his wife, and their two young sons moved to Pittsburgh in October 1947. When he arrived at his new place of employment, his high hopes were quickly deflated. He had expected to set up a large research facility at the Municipal Hospital, which was located next to the university. Instead, he was given a small and cramped section of the hospital basement. He had made his decision, though, and he decided to remain in Pittsburgh and do the job he had been hired to do.

Salk began his influenza research with enthusiasm, despite his cramped working conditions. He also started making plans to expand the laboratory and build it into the type of facility he wanted, although he did not know where the money would come from. A few months later, when a distinguished gentleman paid him a visit, Salk knew he had found his answer.

Fulfillment of a Dream

The man who visited Salk in late 1947 was Harry M. Weaver, the research director for the National Foundation for Infantile Paralysis. Weaver, a former anatomy professor, had an intense interest in poliomyelitis research. While many others in the field of medical science wanted to focus on finding a cure, Weaver believed that the priority should be on finding a vaccination. Because of all the research that was needed, this presented a challenge. Previous studies

Eager to find a vaccine for polio, the National Foundation for Infantile Paralysis financed Salk's poliomyelitis virus research program.

had shown that there were multiple types of the poliovirus, but no one knew how many there were. The only way a polio vaccine could be effective was if it protected against all of the types. Weaver needed to find someone who was devoted to research, and who would spend whatever time was necessary—possibly even years—to identify the different poliovirus types. Many scientists viewed this kind of "virus typing" as drudgery and had no interest in pursuing it. Weaver acknowledged that the work might be tedious, but he also knew it was necessary before any effective vaccine could be developed.

Weaver had heard about a young medical scientist named Dr. Jonas Salk. He was aware that Salk worked in the basement of Pittsburgh's Municipal Hospital, and that his research had been focused on influenza. Weaver also knew that Salk longed for more independence, more money for research, and a more spacious laboratory in which to work. When Weaver found out that polio patients were being treated in some of the hospital wards where Salk worked—and polio patients meant the availability of virus samples—he believed that he had found the ideal scientist to handle his project.

Weaver presented Salk with an offer that was so attractive it was impossible to refuse. He suggested that Municipal Hospital might be the perfect place to conduct a poliomyelitis virus research program. He proposed a grant of several hundred thousand dollars for the work, and he invited Salk to head up the program. Salk was thrilled. Later, he described his reaction to Weaver's offer: "I seized upon that opportunity. It gave me a chance to get funds, to get laboratory facilities, get equipment, and to hire a staff, and to build up something that was not there. It also would provide me with an opportunity to learn about how you work with the poliovirus."[12]

Famous Scientific Minds

In their meeting, Weaver suggested that Salk learn as much as possible about the poliovirus. One way to do this would be to get to know some leading virologists, or scientists who specialize in the study of viruses. In January 1948, Salk attended his first meeting with virologists in Washington, D.C. Some of the most famous names in virus research were there, including Dr. Thomas Francis, Salk's former teacher and mentor, and Dr. Albert Sabin, a respected medical scientist from Cincinnati. At the conference, an immunization committee was formed to supervise the poliovirus project, and both Francis and Sabin were part of the group.

Dr. Albert Sabin (pictured) and other respected virologists formed a committee to supervise Salk's poliovirus project.

Salk was somewhat intimidated by these well-known and respected professionals. He wanted them to accept him because of their stature among other scientists. A thought occurred to him, however, as he listened to them talk. His research was supposed to be done according to their methods. He wondered, what if he came up with better methods? And if his methods were not acceptable to them, how would they react? Salk kept his opinions to himself, but true to his independent nature, he vowed to do the virus research the way he believed it should be done.

A Brand New Space

Salk returned to Pittsburgh ready and eager to get started.
The national grants to the University of Pittsburgh School of
Medicine totaled about two hundred thousand dollars per year,
which was an enormous sum at that time. Municipal Hospital
gave Salk additional space in the basement for his laboratory,
plus two upper floors. Yet he still needed more money.
Extensive renovations were necessary, and grant money could
not be used for construction costs. With the help of the medical school dean, Salk was able to obtain additional funds from
local sources. This money allowed him to transform what was
a cramped, inadequate area into a spacious, modern, and
well-equipped laboratory.

It did not surprise anyone that Salk undertook the renovation
project with the same enthusiasm he showed for everything he
did. When it was possible to begin work on the hospital space,
Salk took charge, as Donna Salk later explained: "He designed
the new laboratories himself. He had the first and final and in-
between words on everything from electrical outlets to paint to
plumbing to office furniture. He not only knew what was on the
floors but was intimately acquainted with the undersides of the
desks. He can't work any other way."[13] As work progressed on the
new laboratories, Salk hired a team of researchers.

Focus on the Poliovirus

During 1949, Salk and his team identified and categorized the
different types of poliovirus. They experimented on monkeys,
which they kept housed in a "monkey colony" on the second
floor of the hospital. At that time, it was believed that the
poliovirus could only grow in living nerve tissue, such as in the
brains of live monkeys. No one had figured out how to make
the virus grow any other way. Because only tiny amounts of
virus could be extracted from the monkeys' brains, hundreds
of animals were needed for the experiments.

Opposite: *Salk used his new funding to build a modern
laboratory equipped with everything he and his researchers
needed.*

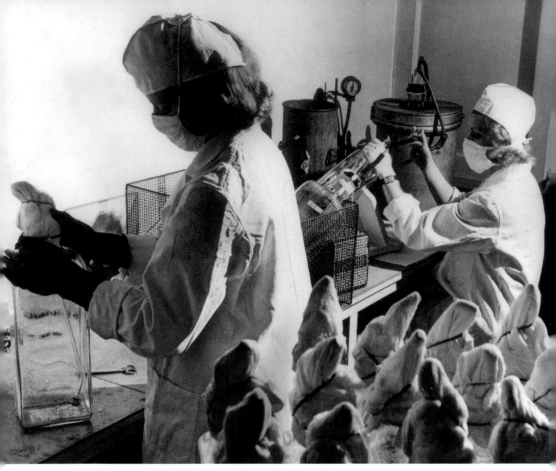

In 1949, Boston doctor John Enders discovered the poliovirus could be grown in test tubes. This discovery enabled researchers like Salk to grow the virus more quickly.

Then, a discovery in 1949 by Boston's Dr. John Enders changed everything. Enders and two other scientists successfully grew poliovirus in test tubes, using human tissue. This was remarkable in the scientific world because it proved that the virus could be grown in ways other than just inside live test animals. It would eliminate the need for so many monkeys, and it would also mean that poliovirus could be grown more quickly.

From Research to Vaccine

Salk was excited about Enders's discovery, and he knew it would make a huge difference in how his research was conducted. Still, the work was both tedious and slow. It was necessary for him and his researchers to sort through more than a hundred virus samples in order to identify the different types. After many months of work, they finally were able to confirm that there were three strains (types) of poliovirus: Brunhilde, Lansing, and Leon. These later became commonly known as type I, type II, and type III.

Once Salk's team had identified the three types of poliovirus, they inactivated them with formalin, a solution made from the chemical formaldehyde. Then they used the killed viruses to create different versions of a vaccine. As their research progressed, Salk became convinced that a vaccine to prevent poliomyelitis was more possible than ever.

In June 1950, Salk wrote to Weaver and discussed his team's progress. His letter described the research methods they had used, which were based on Enders's findings. Salk also informed Weaver of his intent to use killed viruses to make an experimental vaccine, which he believed was very close to completion. At first, Weaver was skeptical because he believed Salk was rushing things. Then in July, he helped Salk prepare a

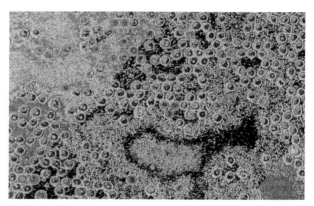

Salk verified three strains of polio and soon developed several possible vaccines from the killed viruses.

proposal for the National Foundation for Infantile Paralysis, in which Salk requested additional funds for his work on vaccines.

For the rest of the year, Salk and his team continued their research. They also prepared for the vaccine experiments that would begin as soon as they received the grant money from the foundation. According to Elsie Ward, one of Salk's research technicians, the mood in the laboratory during that time was

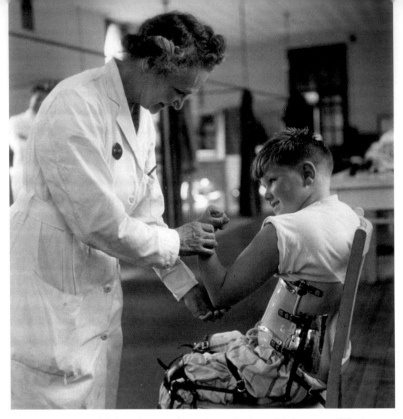

Salk visits to children's wards at hospitals, which were filled with sick and paralyzed polio victims, intensified his search for a cure.

one of excitement: "It was such pure joy to come to work in the morning. Every day brought new progress. To look into the microscope and see what we saw was a great thrill. Dr. Salk was in the lab morning, afternoon, and night. He couldn't wait to see what was going to happen."[14]

By this time, polio had become a terrifying epidemic, and the development of a vaccine was a priority for many scientists. The hospitals were filled with sick and paralyzed children, and the situation had grown desperate. One nurse at Municipal Hospital described the children's ward: "It was an atmosphere of grief, terror, and helpless rage. It was horrible. I remember a high school boy weeping because he was completely paralyzed and couldn't move a hand to kill himself. . . . I remember a little girl who lay motionless for days with her eyes closed. . . . And I can remember how the staff used to kid Dr. Salk—kidding in earnest—telling him to hurry up and do something."[15]

A Distinguished Honor

Salk's intention was definitely to "do something." By now he was the father of three sons; his third son, Jonathan, was born in 1950. Each year, thousands of children continued to be stricken with polio. In 1950 alone, there were nearly thirty-five thousand new victims, and 75 percent were under the age of twenty-one. Salk and his team were determined to help put an end to the crippling disease. They also remained convinced that the only answer to a safe and effective polio vaccine was one that used killed viruses.

In September 1951, Salk was asked to speak at the Second International Poliomyelitis Congress in Copenhagen, Denmark. He traveled by ship, and he was joined on the voyage by Enders, Sabin, and other notable scientists. Salk was pleasantly surprised when Enders, during his own presentation, credited

Basil O'Connor (center), the president of the National Foundation for Infantile Paralysis, agreed to fund Salk's killed-virus vaccine.

Salk for experiments that were paving the way toward a polio vaccine. When Sabin spoke, however, he did not praise Salk. Instead, he warned against "undue optimism." Salk resented Sabin's negative words and from that point on, the relationship between the two scientists was uncomfortable and strained.

During the voyage home from Europe, Salk became acquainted with Basil O'Connor, who was president of the National Foundation for Infantile Paralysis. Salk was invited to join O'Connor's table for dinner one night, an invitation he gladly accepted. During dinner, Salk was introduced to Bettyann Culver, O'Connor's daughter, who had recently been stricken with polio. O'Connor was impressed with many things about Salk, but one thing that especially touched him was the way Salk managed to lift Bettyann's spirits. The two men spent a great deal of time together on the trip home, and they later became good friends.

Back to Work

By the time the voyage ended, O'Connor had developed a great admiration for Salk's passion, brilliance, and enthusiasm. He therefore gave Salk exciting news: The foundation, which had funded Salk's research, would also finance his development of a killed-virus vaccine.

Back in his laboratory, Salk worked on his experiments with a renewed sense of purpose. The funding for his research was now guaranteed, and he was confident that the discovery of a poliomyelitis vaccine was only a matter of time. He knew, though, that it would be a while before any vaccine was ready to be tested on humans. First, he had to find which strains of the killed virus would produce the most antibodies in monkeys; higher levels of antibodies meant greater immunity to disease. Yet, even if he found it, the real trick would be to make sure it had the same effect on human beings.

The Race for a Vaccine

Salk and his team worked out the many details of growing the virus, including how to produce the greatest possible amount. They also tested different amounts of chemicals—too much

New funds renewed Salk's confidence as he and his team worked tirelessly to develop a vaccine that could be safely tested on humans.

could cause the virus to be useless, and too little would not inactivate the virus. In his book, *Breakthrough: The Saga of Jonas Salk* biographer Richard Carter describes how critical this process was: "He had to decide the proportions in which virus and Formalin should be combined. And at what temperature should the reaction take place? And how long should it last? And how could he be sure that any single batch of supposedly inactivated virus was really inactivated, thoroughly harmless? Suppose it contained a few living particles, enough to kill a child?"[16]

The research and experiments continued throughout the winter of 1951 and into 1952. Salk and his team worked tirelessly. They figured out ways to grow the poliovirus at a faster rate, which was extremely important. Huge amounts of the virus would be needed to make enough vaccine for human

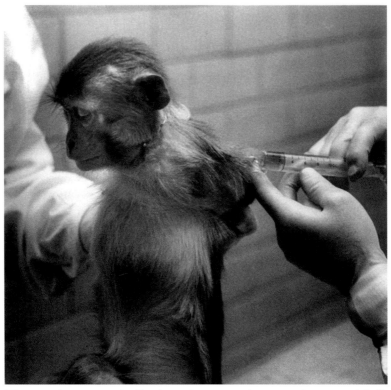

The vaccine proved effective when tested on monkeys, and Salk hoped it would have the same result when tried on humans.

testing. Once they had prepared a solution from the killed virus, they injected it into monkeys. The monkeys showed no signs of illness, and within twenty-one days they had developed high levels of antibodies. The team declared their work a major success. The next step would be to test the experimental vaccine on humans.

In April 1952, Salk attended a conference of the immunization committee in New York. He gave a detailed presentation to the group about his team's success, and he spoke about how their findings would be the basis for a human experiment. The group's warm response indicated their support. Even Sabin, who had been pursuing his own live-virus research, spoke positively about Salk's presentation. He was quick to caution the group, however, that while he believed the research should continue, it showed "how much more has to be learned before one can even think of beginning to know what kind of test to try in human beings. . . ."[17]

Vaccinating Children

O'Connor and Weaver disagreed that tests on humans should wait. The polio epidemic was growing worse and if something could be done, they believed it needed to be done without delay. They gave Salk their approval to perform the first test on children at the D.T. Watson Home for Crippled Children. The result was the successful experiment that was performed during the summer of 1952.

In 1952, Salk brought his vaccine to a home for crippled children and administered the first successful human inoculations.

During the rest of 1952, and for the first few months of 1953, Salk conducted more tests, which were also kept secret from the public. He inoculated other children at the Watson Home, and performed inoculations at the Polk State School, a Pennsylvania facility for the mentally retarded. As with previous tests, no one who was vaccinated suffered any ill effects. By the time these tests were complete, it had become obvious that Salk's experimental vaccine was both safe and effective.

On March 26, 1953, Salk made his discovery known to the American people. He appeared on a special radio broadcast, entitled "The Scientist Speaks for Himself," and spoke to the nation about his ongoing research, testing, and the vaccine. His message was one of confidence and hope. He made it clear, though, that it was necessary to be cautious because more tests were needed before the vaccine was ready for the public.

Salk was unprepared for the reaction to his radio address. The next day, newspapers carried the story as front-page news, and soon after that Salk was flooded with requests for interviews. He became frustrated with all the media attention, as he later expressed: "It was impossible. It was outrageous. No work could be done with those people stumbling all over the place."[18] The media's reaction was not the only thing that disturbed Salk. Some scientists and doctors sharply criticized his radio appearance. In the medical world, that kind of public announcement was considered both undignified and unprofessional.

Complex Preparations

The media attention died down within a month or two, and Salk could again focus on preparing his vaccine for more tests. In April 1953, he inoculated his wife and their three sons, who were nine, six, and three years old. He also continued to do inoculations on more children at the Watson Home. As before, there were no problems caused by the vaccine, and it successfully created protective antibodies in the children's blood.

To test the vaccine on a larger scale, Salk, O'Connor, and others proposed a national field trial. Between mid-1953 and early 1954, plans were finalized for the nationwide tests. This preparation was a long and involved process. The vaccine

Salk immunized his wife and three children after the tests he conducted in 1952 and 1953 proved his vaccine was safe and effective.

needed to be prepared in very large quantities, and it was essential that it be of acceptable quality. It was also a challenge to obtain the necessary approvals, gather children for the tests, choose the test sites, and find enough people to help.

Some scientists were very much opposed to the field trial. Sabin, for one, was especially outspoken and critical. In a presentation to the American Medical Association, he stressed his continued belief that Salk's killed-virus vaccine could not be effective: "The basic information that one should have about a vaccine before it is tested in human beings is not yet available. . . . The ultimate goal for the prevention of poliomyelitis is immunization with 'living' . . . virus. . . ."[19] Sabin also wrote to Salk and said that he believed the killed-virus vaccine would not be effective, and that it would ruin Salk's career. The years-long conflict between the two scientists grew more heated.

Sabin was a highly respected scientist who had received his own funding from the National Foundation for Infantile Paralysis. In spite of this, however, the foundation was determined to go ahead with the field trial. They believed that the longer they waited, the longer the nation's children would be at risk. Parents of children all over the country agreed. They were tired of living in fear. They knew that another polio season was just months away, and they wanted the dreaded epidemic to end.

The Famous Nationwide Test

Beginning in April 1954 and throughout the summer, nearly 2 million grade school children, called "Polio Pioneers," were inoculated with Salk's vaccine. The field trials were held at 217 test sites in forty-four states around the country and more than three hundred thousand doctors, teachers, nurses, and volunteers provided assistance. It was the largest and most famous field trial ever.

A year went by before all the field trial results were gathered and tabulated. By early April 1955, Francis had compiled the information into a lengthy report. The overall conclusion: The vaccine was as much as 80 to 90 percent effective in preventing polio. This was wonderful news, and all who were involved were overjoyed, as well as relieved. The vaccine really worked. Now it was time to let the public in on the secret.

Announcing the Triumph over Polio

On April 12, 1955, a news conference was held in Ann Arbor, and hundreds of scientists, nonscientists, and news people attended. Francis made the long-awaited announcement: The poliovirus vaccine developed by Dr. Jonas Salk was safe, effective, and potent. Americans would no longer have to fear the disease they had dreaded for decades.

The next day, news headlines all over the United States praised Salk and called him a hero. Throughout the country, church bells rang, horns blew, fire sirens wailed, and people

In 1954, doctors, nurses, and teachers inoculated 2 million children with Salk's vaccine in the largest and most famous field trial ever.

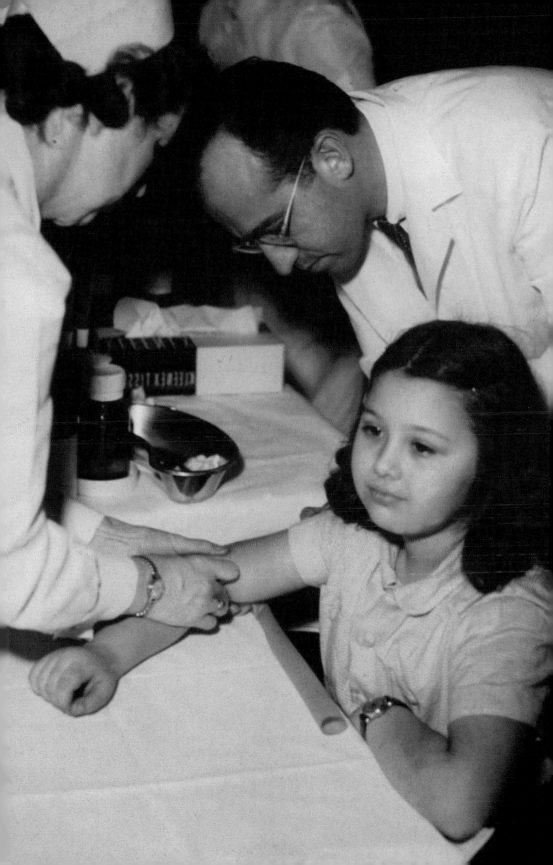

The nation hailed Salk as a hero and President Dwight D. Eisenhower (at podium) presented the scientist with a medal for his groundbreaking vaccine.

shouted their praises. Salk was featured in newspapers, on magazine covers, on the radio, and on television. He was even invited to the White House to receive a medal from Dwight D. Eisenhower, the president of the United States. Overnight, the name Jonas Salk had become one of the most famous names in history.

Yet Salk did not seek fame or celebrity status, nor did he think of himself as a hero. He was a modest man whose only wish was for the vaccine to be made available to people so it could protect them from polio. He even refused to get a patent for his vaccine, which would have given him the exclusive rights to own and manufacture it. In fact, when Salk was asked who owned the polio vaccine, he replied, "I'd say it belongs to everyone. I mean, could you patent the sun?"[20]

A Heartwarming Welcome

Following the news conference, Salk returned to Pittsburgh with his wife and three sons, who had accompanied him to Ann Arbor. They were met at the airport by a huge welcoming committee that included city officials, friends, coworkers, and the news media. Donna Salk described the ride home in the mayor's limousine, escorted by police on motorcycles: "Home we went, the sirens screaming and the cavalcade going in the wrong direction down a one-way street. When we got home we found a police guard posted at the house. The place was full of mail. Letters from everywhere on earth, from polio patients and the parents of polio patients, some of them enclosing dollars or shillings or francs. . . ."[21] Truckloads of fan mail continued to arrive every day, and Salk also received a 208-foot telegram that was signed by more than seven thousand people.

Salk was very grateful to everyone for their gratitude and support. As always, though, he despised the spotlight and he wanted nothing more than to go back to work. He later described how it felt to be in the center of all the attention: "I felt myself very much like someone in the eye of a hurricane, because all this swirling was going on around me. It was at that moment that everything changed."[22]

From Triumph to Tragedy

As soon as the public became aware of Salk's vaccine, there was a nationwide demand for it. The National Foundation for Infantile Paralysis had expected this, and O'Connor had arranged for several drug companies to manufacture the vaccine. Within two weeks, about 5 million children around the country had been inoculated, and plans were underway to inoculate millions more. Then a crisis happened, and the program suddenly came to a halt. A large batch of vaccine that had been made by Cutter Laboratories had been contaminated with live poliovirus instead of killed virus. As a result, more than two hundred children were stricken with polio. Fifty of them were paralyzed, and eleven died.

All use of the vaccine was stopped until the problem could be found. Salk was devastated. What had happened was not his

ENTRANCE
for polio shots

fault, but he knew the incident would cause people to lose trust in his vaccine. Also, the inoculation program would be delayed, which he feared would prevent children from being vaccinated before the onset of the polio season. He felt as though all his efforts and progress had been set back several years.

After the public announcement that Salk's poliovirus vaccine was both safe and effective, millions of children across the country received inoculations.

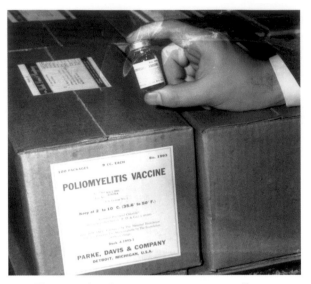

The vaccination program temporarily stopped until a contaminated batch of the vaccine was identified and taken out of circulation.

The Inoculations Resume

Once the problem was traced to Cutter, the defective vaccine was taken out of circulation. On May 27, 1955, the U.S. Surgeon General announced that the inoculation program could be resumed, and the nationwide program started again.

By the end of 1955, more than 10 million children had been inoculated, and polio cases in the United States had dropped by 25 percent. Two years later, more than half of all Americans under the age of forty had been inoculated, and the number of polio cases dropped nearly 90 percent. The disease that had gripped the nation in fear since 1916 was on its way to becoming extinct.

A Live-Virus Vaccine

In spite of the proven success of Salk's polio vaccine, Sabin held fast to his belief that a vaccine made from live viruses would be superior. He had been working on one of his own, and he resented the fact that Salk had finished his vaccine first. Also, he was bitter about all the attention and fame that Salk had received. By 1959, Sabin had his vaccine ready to test. Unlike Salk's, Sabin's vaccine was given orally on a lump of sugar, which he believed was preferable to a needle injection. Also, he claimed that his live-virus vaccine would provide immunity for

Albert Sabin developed a live-virus polio vaccine that could be given orally on a sugar cube (pictured).

a much longer time than one developed with killed viruses. It was not known for sure how long Salk's vaccine would provide immunity, and periodic booster shots were recommended.

Between 1959 and 1961, Sabin tested his vaccine in Russia, where there had been polio epidemics since the early 1900s.

Based on Russian data, the tests were declared a success by world health experts, and by late 1961, Sabin's vaccine was licensed for use in the United States. It also received the endorsement of the American Medical Association—which meant the esteemed group of medical professionals recommended it over Salk's vaccine. For Salk, O'Connor, and all the others who had worked so hard to make the killed-virus vaccine a reality, this was a terrible blow. Not only did they think the decision was unfair and unjust, but they also believed it was dangerous because of the risks involved with live viruses. Nevertheless, Sabin's vaccine was made available all over the country, and it became the vaccine of choice.

Sabin strongly defended his vaccine, which was the top choice nationwide until outbreaks of paralytic polio began to appear.

Those who doubted the safety of Sabin's vaccine soon had their worst fears confirmed. Within four months after it became available in America, new polio cases were reported. By June 1964, over one hundred new cases of paralytic polio had been confirmed. In spite of that, the medical organizations that had endorsed Sabin's work continued to recommend his vaccine over Salk's. They believed the benefits of the live-virus vaccine far outweighed the risk that a small number of people might contract polio. This infuriated O'Connor, who remarked: "Let's stop pretending. The Sabin vaccine is causing cases of paralysis. And the government does nothing about it but pussyfoot. I wonder whether anybody cares about anything anymore."[23]

Moving on

Eventually, worldwide medical experts recommended that children be inoculated with both types of vaccines—first a killed-virus vaccine to create immunity, and then a live-virus one for longer-term protection. Salk strongly disagreed with this type of thinking. He also questioned the logic of Sabin's vaccine being recommended at all: "The public ought to have a choice: both vaccines immunize equally well; one occasionally causes paralysis."[24] For the rest of his life, Salk never stopped believing that vaccines would only be safe if they contained no trace of live viruses.

During the late 1950s, Salk continued his virus research at the University of Pittsburgh and spent time refining his polio vaccine. He also served on the expert advisory panel of the World Health Organization on viral diseases.

By 1960, Salk was ready to explore new challenges. At the age of forty-six, he had accomplished amazing things, yet there was still much more that he wanted to do. For years he had dreamed about starting his own research institute. He envisioned a place where scientists and brilliant people in other fields could work together, perform research, and share their knowledge for the benefit of humanity. Salk was interested in art as well as science, as he explained: "I think that there is both an art and a science to what we do. The art of science is as important as so-called technical science. You need both. It's this combination that must be recognized and acknowledged and valued."[25] Salk's vision was that his new institute would combine the best of both science and art. He believed a place that inspired people to be creative would also lead them to explore new scientific challenges.

A Lifelong Dream

To many scientists, Salk's idea sounded like a lofty one, even quite odd. He described what some of them told him when he first spoke about it: "People questioned it and said, 'Scientists work in laboratories, they look into microscopes, they work in basements.' And I said, 'Yes that's true. I did all that myself but I want to see what happens if you do the experiment the other way. How do we know what might happen, unless we try?'"[26] The reason Salk's idea seemed so strange at the time was because nothing like it had ever existed before. Nowhere else was there a research institute where different types of scientists and nonscientists worked together, under one roof, and shared their ideas with each other. It was simply unheard of. Anyone who knew Jonas Salk, however, knew that he did things according to what he believed was right.

For more than a year, Salk traveled around the country to find the perfect location for his institute. He found exactly what he wanted in La Jolla, California, a suburb of San Diego. The people of San Diego generously donated twenty-seven acres of land for the institute's headquarters. The National Foundation for Infantile Paralysis gave Salk a grant for start-up funds, and also promised Salk continued financial support.

In 1963, the Salk Institute for Biological Studies began operations in temporary quarters. Salk assembled an extraordinary staff, which included some of the most brilliant and respected scientists, physicians, and mathematicians in the country. Several of these people had won the Nobel Prize. Salk became the director, and from the beginning, he was passionate about what his institute would achieve. One colleague explained this years later: "The Institute is the blood of his blood and the soul of his soul. It is his life. He wants it to be just right in every particular. His definition of 'right' may differ from yours or mine, of course, and so may his notion of how to achieve 'right.' But we cherish him. He is the only man in the world

---

Salk realized a lifelong dream when he opened the Salk Institute, a research setting where scientists and nonscientists could collaborate on new discoveries, in La Jolla, California.

who could have put this Institute together . . . and the reasons why he has given years of his life to it are good reasons. The scientific and social issues which interest him are important."[27]

There was another reason why Salk was so pleased with his new research facility: He could finally escape from the public eye and focus on his work as a scientist. Although ten years had passed since his polio vaccine was first announced, he was still viewed as a celebrity and he wanted no part of it. He explained this during a television interview: "I sometimes think that the idea of creating an institute was to create a shelter for myself. I still hope . . . that I can somehow, some way, find a refuge here, find respite from the strong tendency and temptation and desire from others to have me function as a public figure rather than as an individual. . . ."[28]

A Place Where Creativity Thrives

Salk's institute provided him with the privacy he had wanted for so long. As construction on the new buildings progressed, he was actively involved—just as he had been during the renovation of his Pittsburgh laboratory nearly twenty years before. The work was finally complete in 1967, and the new headquarters, a cluster of elegant structures that overlooked the Pacific Ocean, was ready for operation. Salk described it as a "marvelous architectural setting, where people could do scientific work in a work of art."[29] Salk's institute was a place where people could think, dream, and share ideas. It was a place where they could be creative, where laboratories and other work areas were designed especially for those who worked in them. The new Salk Institute was truly unique— there was nothing else like it in the world.

Art and Science Together

To finally see his lifelong dream become a reality was a marvelous thing for Salk. He had worked very hard, for a very long time, to get to this point, and his surroundings were proof of that. He had achieved exactly what he had set out to achieve. Yet he was far from finished. From the time he was a young boy, when his mother constantly pushed him toward new

The elegant architecture of the Salk Institute adds to its atmosphere of creativity and professional cameraderie.

challenges, Salk had driven himself to seek, explore, and discover. This was how he lived his whole life, as he once expressed: "I feel that the greatest reward for success is the opportunity to do more."[30]

Throughout his career, Salk had always been happiest when he was in the laboratory, and he was delighted to be back there again. In the late 1960s, he continued his research on the human immune system. He began to study autoimmunity, an abnormal condition in which the body's immune system attacks and destroys its own healthy cells. He believed this would lead to new knowledge of such diseases as arthritis and multiple sclerosis (MS). He was also curious about why people's bodies sometimes rejected skin grafts, tumors, or transplanted organs or tissue. His research in this area, he believed, could lead to progress with heart and kidney transplant surgeries.

This was also a time of major change in Salk's personal life. In 1968, he and his wife, Donna, were divorced after nearly thirty years of marriage. Two years later, Salk met Francoise Gilot, a French artist and former long-time companion to Pablo Picasso, the famous Spanish painter. Soon after Salk and Gilot met in Paris, they were married.

After a divorce from his first wife, Salk married French artist Francoise Gilot.

The Next Decade

In Gilot, Salk found not only a marriage partner, but also a friend who encouraged his desire to be creative. He found their marriage to be extremely rewarding, and he admired many things about her, as he explained: "It's not only her artistic qualities, but her qualities as a human being and as a powerful intellect. That has been one of the great good fortunes in my life and my career."[31] Gilot helped expand Salk's knowledge about the world of art, and she encouraged his interest in it. He praised her as a magnificent artist, as well as a wonderful writer.

Throughout the 1970s, Salk continued his research on the immune system, and he began to study diseases such as cancer and multiple sclerosis. Also during the 1970s, he returned to polio research because the debate over live- versus killed-virus polio vaccines had reemerged. Even though Sabin's vaccine had helped to wipe out polio in the United States, it caused about ten new cases of paralytic polio each year. Salk, as well as others who believed only in the killed-virus vaccine, once again raised the question: Since the Salk vaccine had been proven effective and safe, why was a live-virus vaccine still the recommended choice? Several lawsuits were filed by people who had caught polio from the Sabin vaccine, and some of the victims were awarded millions of dollars. Salk often served as an advisor and expert witness in these court cases.

The Last Years

Salk's polio research continued throughout the 1980s. He worked to refine his polio vaccine so it would provide longer-lasting immunity. He also developed a new version—called E-IPV—that could be blended with other vaccines for the prevention of diphtheria, tetanus, and pertussis (DPT). This helped simplify vaccinations in children because they could get one inoculation instead of several. Pharmaceutical companies in France, Canada, and the Netherlands manufactured the new vaccine, and Salk worked closely with them in the development process.

In the late 1980s, Salk turned his attention in a new direction: the prevention and treatment of acquired immuno-deficiency syndrome, or AIDS. The vaccine he envisioned would be very different from the polio vaccine he had developed. This would be used on people who had already been infected with HIV, the human immunodeficiency

In his final years of research, Salk worked to develop a vaccine that would prevent the HIV virus from developing into AIDS.

virus that caused AIDS. He believed this type of vaccine could help stop the infection from developing into AIDS. Once again, he firmly believed that the only safe and effective vaccine was one that was made with killed viruses. In 1987, Salk formed a separate company called Immune Response Corporation, and its purpose was to develop Salk's AIDS vaccine.

As had been the case so often in the past, many scientists doubted Salk's approach. They did not share his belief in a killed-virus vaccine. Also, they were not convinced that a vaccine could help prevent a disease if people already had HIV in their blood. For much of his life, Salk had dealt with this type of criticism and once again, it did not stop him. His response this time was to say: "We want desperately now to move forward. You can fail only if you stop too soon."[32]

The Loss of a Hero

Salk developed an experimental AIDS vaccine. In 1991, he announced that he intended to inject himself with the vaccine—just as he had with his polio vaccine many years before. It is not known, however, whether he actually followed through with the inoculation. He was refining the vaccine right up until his death on June 23, 1995, when he died of congestive heart failure. He was eighty years old.

Salk was buried in La Jolla, California, the place he had selected for his institute more than thirty years before. A memorial at the institute gives tribute to the man who devoted his entire life toward helping his fellow human beings. It includes his own statement that reads: "Hope lies in dreams, in imagination and in the courage of those who dare to make dreams into reality."

Salk's Legacy

Jonas Salk never won a Nobel Prize, and he was never elected to the National Academy of Sciences. He was often scorned by his fellow scientists, and was even ridiculed by some of them. Still, he was a legend in the field of medical science.

Throughout his life, Salk published more than one hundred scientific publications and books, and he received numerous

Although Salk received many honors and awards, his only concern was to conduct medical research for the good of humanity.

awards. Some of his honors included the Albert Lasker Award by the American Public Health Association in New York; the Robert Koch Medal; the Mellon Institute Award; a U.S. Presidential Citation; and a Congressional Gold Medal, just to name a few. Also, he was honored by the French government and received honorary degrees from universities in the United States, Britain, Israel, Italy, and the Philippines.

Yet Salk was never concerned with honors or awards or fame. He was only interested in one thing: making a difference in the world on behalf of humanity. He had very specific ideas about what he believed was right, and he never stopped fighting for those ideas.

Many people have praised Salk—his life as well as his work—but perhaps the best testimonial about him was given by Dr. Francis Crick, a recipient of the Nobel prize and current president of the Salk Institute. In Salk's memory, Crick said: "Few have made one discovery that has benefited humanity so greatly. Jonas was a man who, right to his last day, was actively in pursuit of another."[33]

IMPORTANT DATES

1890s	First known polio outbreak in the United States in Vermont.
Early 1900s	European scientists determine that polio is a virus that is spread through direct contact.
1914	Jonas Edward Salk is born in New York City.
1916	Major polio epidemic breaks out in states along the East Coast; by the end of summer, more than thirty thousand cases are reported in twenty-six states.
1918	Spanish influenza pandemic claims more than 20 million people, of whom more than a half-million were Americans.
1934	Salk graduates from City College of New York and enters medical school at New York University School of Medicine.
1935	American physician John Kolmer attempts to develop polio vaccine; because of his experiments, some children suffer paralysis and death.
1939	Salk graduates from medical school; one day later, he marries Donna Lindsay.
1940	Begins medical internship at Mount Sinai Hospital in New York City.
1942	Joins Dr. Thomas Francis Jr. at University of Michigan School of Public Health in Ann Arbor.
1943	Begins work with the U.S. Army Influenza Commission.
1944	Son Peter is born.
1945	Travels to Germany to organize diagnostic laboratories for the prevention of influenza epidemics.
1946	Promoted to assistant professor position at University of Michigan School of Public Health.
1947	Son Darrell is born; Salk accepts position at University of Pittsburgh School of Medicine as research professor and head of the virus research laboratory; agrees to conduct poliomyelitis virus research funded by the National Foundation for Infantile Paralysis.
1949	Boston Dr. John Enders and two other scientists discover how to grow poliovirus in test tubes, using human tissue.
1950	Son Jonathan is born; polio epidemic worsens—thiry-three thousand new victims in one year, 75 percent of whom are under the age of twenty-one.
1951	Salk travels to Copenhagen, Denmark, to attend Second International Poliomyelitis Congress; becomes friends with Basil O'Connor, who agrees to fund development of killed-virus polio vaccine.
1952	Experimental polio vaccine is complete; in secret, vaccine is tested on children at D.T. Watson Home for Crippled Children in Pittsburgh, Pennsylvania.

1952–1953	Continued testing of vaccine.
1953	Salk announces vaccine to the American people in radio broadcast entitled "The Scientist Speaks for Himself."
1954	Nationwide field trial of Salk vaccine; nearly 2 million children are inoculated.
1955	News conference in Ann Arbor to announce the successful test and the first vaccine proven to prevent polio.
1961	Live-virus vaccine developed by Dr. Albert Sabin licensed for use in the United States, and endorsed by the American Medical Association.
1963	Salk Institute for Biological Studies opens in temporary quarters in La Jolla, California.
1967	New institute headquarters complete.
1968	Divorced from Donna Salk, his wife of nearly thirty years.
1970	Meets and marries French artist Francoise Gilot.
1970s	Continues research on the human immune system, and begins to study cancer and MS; returns to polio research, and serves as advisor and expert witness in lawsuits filed by polio victims.
1980s	Develops new polio vaccine to be blended with other children's vaccines; begins research into AIDS.
1987	Forms new company, Immune Response Corporation, to work toward development of an AIDS vaccine.
1995	Dies at age eighty and is buried in La Jolla.

FOR MORE INFORMATION

BOOKS

John Bankston, *Jonas Salk and the Polio Vaccine*. Bear, DE: Mitchell Lane, 2002. A book about Salk's life, from his childhood through his adult years. Covers his work, his relationships with other scientists, and his many accomplishments.

Nina Gilden Seavey, Jane S. Smith, and Paul Wagner, *A Paralyzing Fear: The Triumph over Polio in America*. New York: TV Books, 1998. A very informative book about polio, including information on Salk, Sabin, and other scientists who studied the disease. Also includes personal testimonials by people who were victims of polio.

Victoria Sherrow, *Jonas Salk*. New York: Facts On File, 1993. A biography of Salk that focuses primarily on his development of a vaccine for polio. Includes a history of disease research and information about some other prominent scientists.

Jane S. Smith, *Patenting the Sun: Polio and the Salk Vaccine*. New York: W. Morrow, 1990. A story about the people and events behind the development of Salk's polio vaccine. Starts with a profile of Franklin Roosevelt's battle against paralysis, and describes one of the greatest accomplishments of the twentieth century: the defeat of poliomyelitis.

FOR MORE INFORMATION

WEBSITES

The Hall of Science & Exploration
www.achievement.org
An excellent, comprehensive site, with a biography of Jonas Salk and a personal interview. Includes audio/video clips and a nice collection of photos.

A Science Odyssey: People and Discoveries: Jonas Salk
www.pbs.org
A site by the Public Broadcasting Service (PBS) that focuses on Salk, and is part of a collection of stories about prominent twentieth-century scientists.

GLOSSARY

AIDS: acquired immunodeficiency syndrome, a disease caused by a virus that destroys the body's immune system.

Antibodies: Substances in the blood that help fight infection and disease.

Autoimmunity: A condition in which the body's immune system mistakenly attacks and destroys certain types of its own healthy cells.

Epidemic: An outbreak of a disease that spreads within a region or country.

Formalin: A solution made from the chemical formaldehyde.

HIV: Human immunodeficiency virus, the virus that causes AIDS.

Immune system: The body's system of organs and cells that defend it against infection, disease, and foreign substances.

Influenza: A highly infectious viral respiratory disease.

Inoculate: To inject a vaccine into a living thing to protect against disease (also called vaccinate).

Killed-virus vaccine: A vaccine that is made from a virus that has been inactivated, usually through the use of chemicals (as opposed to a live-virus vaccine, which uses living virus material).

Nobel Prize: A prestigious award that is given each year for superior accomplishments in physics, chemistry, physiology or medicine, literature, economics, and the promotion of world peace.

Pandemic: An epidemic that spreads throughout the world.

Patent: A document issued by the federal government that grants an inventor exclusive rights to manufacture or sell an invention.

Poliomyelitis (polio): An infectious disease that can lead to paralysis or death.

Poliovirus: The type of virus that can cause polio.

Strain: Another word for "type," as in a particular type, or strain, of virus.

Toxin: A poisonous substance.

Toxoid: A toxin that has been treated with chemicals or radiation so it is no longer harmful, but still causes protective antibodies to form in the blood.

Vaccine: A solution made from killed or live virus material that is used to prevent disease.

Virus: A tiny germ, parasite, or poisonous substance that grows and reproduces in living cells and can lead to disease.

NOTES

1. Quoted in Richard Carter, *Breakthrough: The Saga of Jonas Salk*. New York: Trident Press, 1966, p. 138.
2. Quoted in Carter, *Breakthrough*, p. 139.
3. Quoted in Pat Zacharias, "Conquering the Dreaded Crippler, Polio," Detroit News Online, Rearview Mirror. www.detnews.com.
4. Jonas Salk M.D., interview by Academy of Achievement, The Hall of Science & Exploration, May 16, 1991. www.achievement.org.
5. Salk, Academy of Achievement interview.
6. Salk, Academy of Achievement interview.
7. Quoted in Carter, *Breakthrough*, p. 34.
8. Quoted in Carter, *Breakthrough*, p. 37.
9. Quoted in Carter, *Breakthrough*, p. 38.
10. Quoted in Carter, *Breakthrough*, pp. 45–46.
11. Salk, Academy of Achievement interview.
12. Salk, Academy of Achievement interview.
13. Quoted in Carter, *Breakthrough*, p. 66.
14. Quoted in Carter, *Breakthrough*, p. 106.
15. Quoted in Carter, *Breakthrough*, pp. 107–108.
16. Carter, *Breakthrough*, p. 123.
17. Quoted in Carter, *Breakthrough*, p. 136.
18. Quoted in Carter, *Breakthrough*, p. 166.
19. Quoted in Carter, *Breakthrough*, p. 180.
20. Quoted in Nina Gilden Seavey, Jane S. Smith, and Paul Wagner, *A Paralyzing Fear: The Triumph over Polio in America*, New York: TV Books, 1998, p. 175.
21. Quoted in Carter, *Breakthrough*, p. 288.
22. Salk, Academy of Achievement interview.
23. Quoted in Carter, *Breakthrough*, p. 342.
24. Quoted in Daniel Jack Chasan, "The Polio Paradox," *Science*, April 1986, p. 36.
25. Salk, Academy of Achievement interview.
26. Salk, Academy of Achievement interview.
27. Quoted in Carter, *Breakthrough*, p. 413.
28. Quoted in Dorothy Ducas "Jonas Salk," in Will Yolen and Kenneth Seeman Giniger, eds., *Heroes for Our Times*. Harrisburg, PA: Stackpole, 1968, p. 87.
29. Salk, Academy of Achievement interview.
30. Quoted in "About Jonas Salk," Salk Institute for Biological Studies. www.salk.edu.
31. Salk, Academy of Achievement interview.
32. Quoted in Christine Gorman, "Salk Vaccine for AIDS," *Time*, February 6, 1995, p. 53.
33. Quoted in Harold M. Schmeck Jr., "On This Day: Dr. Jonas Salk, Whose Vaccine Turned Tide on Polio, Dies at 80," New York Times.com, June 24, 1995. www.nytimes.com.

INDEX